The Best Of Haydn

For String Quartet or String Orchestra

Compiled and Edited by
Samuel Applebaum and Paul Paradise

CONTENTS

FOREWORD

For decades the aim of young string players was to become soloists or orchestra players. The last twenty-five years have altered this trend considerably. Chamber music has now become a way of life for a large number of instrumentalists. This does not imply there is a lack of interest in solo and orchestra work; as a matter of fact, our whole musical educational system is based on fine orchestras and band ensembles. However, one cannot overlook the increased interest and enjoyment in chamber music.

This type of musical expression is a complete experience in itself, and each member is only as good as the sum of the other members. The technical values in chamber music are:
1. The development of an acute sense of listening.
2. The opportunity to develop an unusually sensitive type of intonation and blending of dynamics.
3. A maturity in planning the interpretation incorporating the four players.
4. Satisfying the need for individualism.

This album is designed to open the door to string quartet playing. We have chosen movements from the vast output of Haydn string quartets and assembled them according to level of difficulty. Care has been taken to edit each part with contemporary fingerings and bowings. Selections were chosen to provide each player with a meaningful part, and can serve two purposes: 1) to learn some of the more important movements of Haydn's quartets; 2) serve as an encore collection for recital purposes.

A string bass part has been added along with the score so that the album is suitable for string orchestra as well as string quartet.

The Best of Haydn
Menuetto

Op. 2 No. 5

Trio
20
pizz.
arco
p
Menuetto D.C.

Allegretto

Op. 2 No. 5

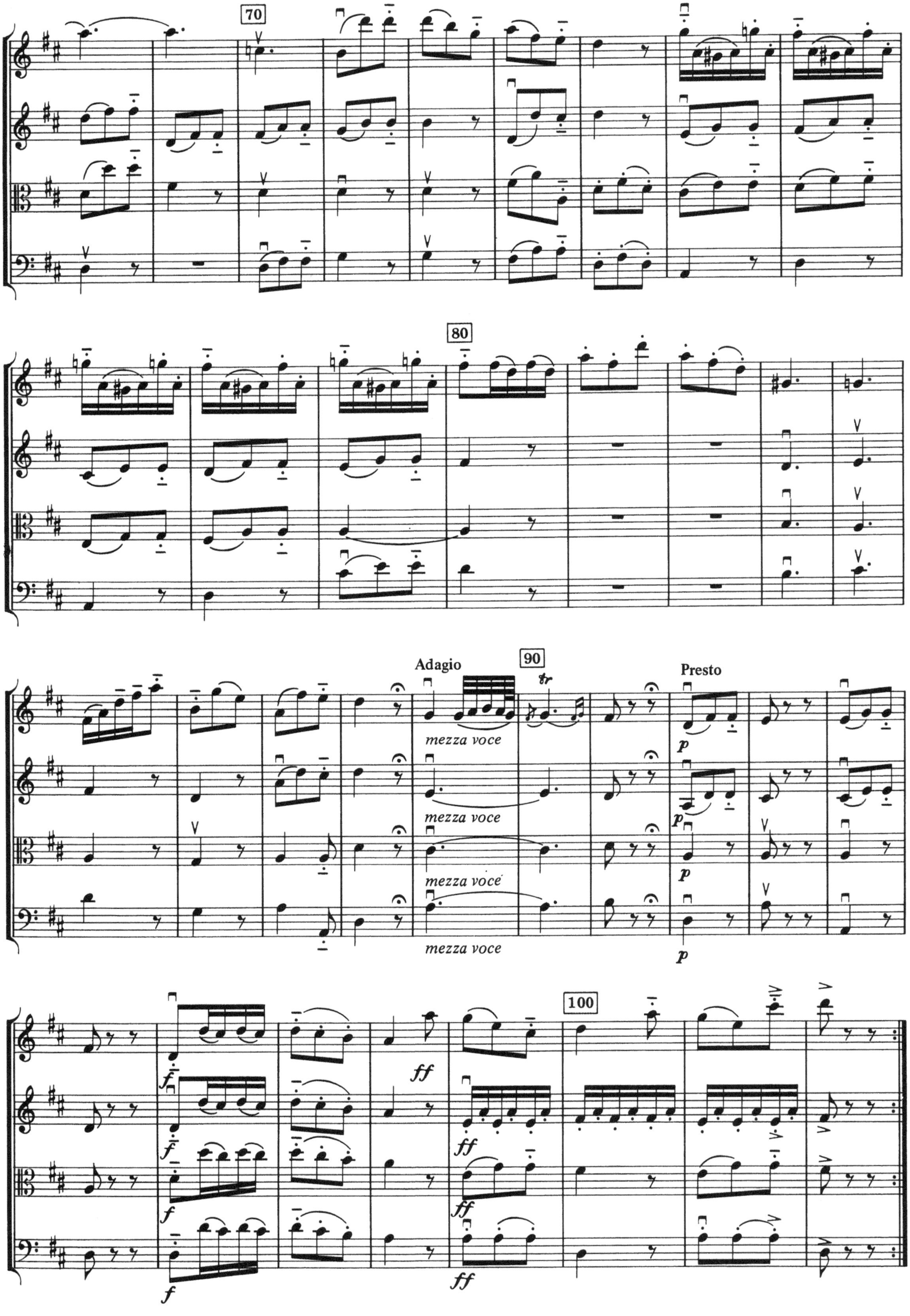
70
80
Adagio
90
Presto
mezza voce
mezza voce
mezza voce
mezza voce
p
p
p
p
100
f
f
f
f
ff
ff
ff
ff

Menuetto

Allegretto

Op. 17 No. 2

Trio
spicc.
spicc.
40
50
dim.
dim.
dim.
dim.
60
Menuetto D.C.

Presto

Op. 1 No. 2

30
f
f
f
f
f
Spicc.
simile
40
p
fp
p
p
fp
p
fp
p

Allegro

Op. 3 No. 6

70
80
90
p
dim.
pp
f
spicc.

100
110
120

Menuetto

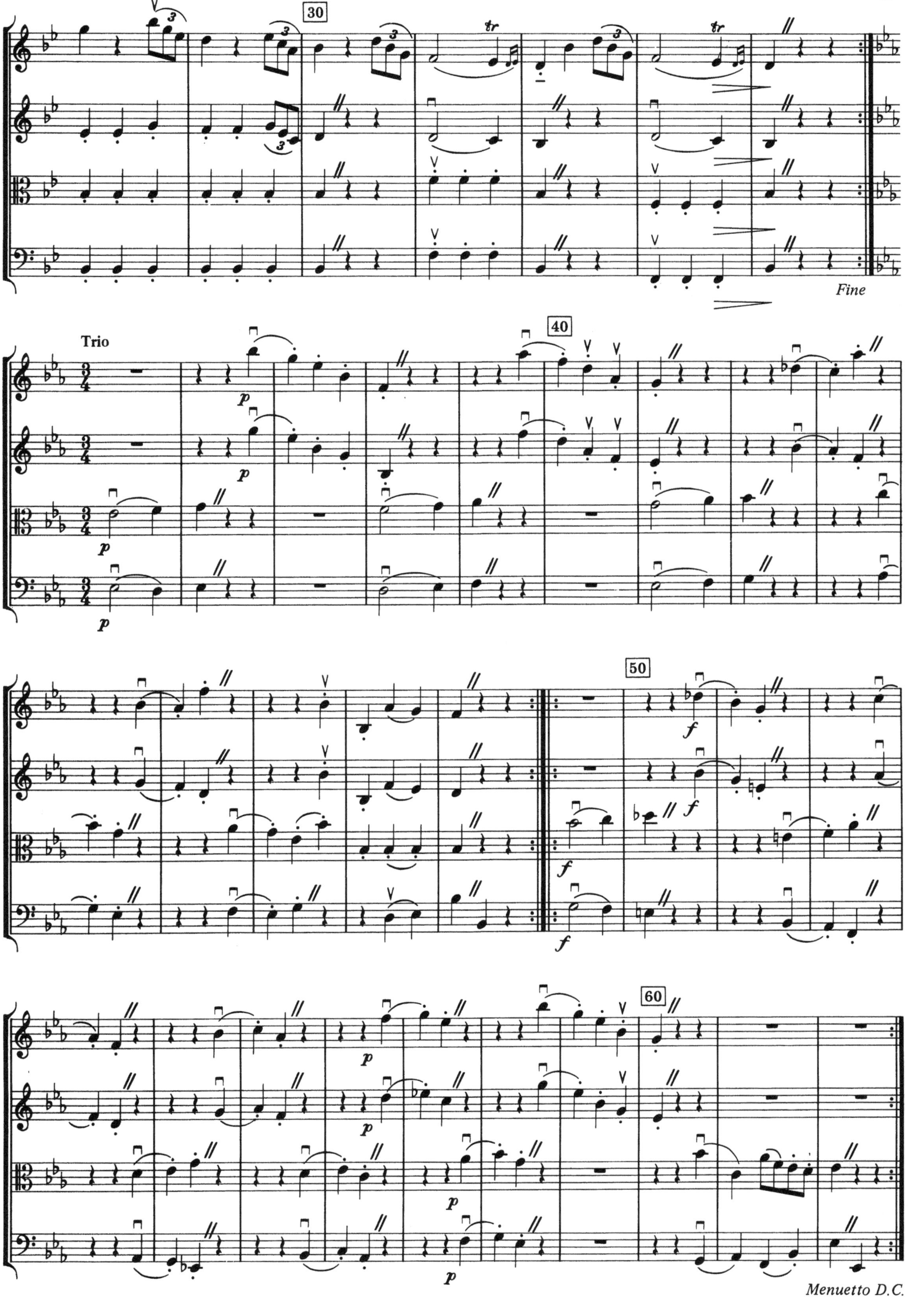
30
tr
tr
Fine
Trio
p
40
50
f
60
p
Menuetto D.C.

Presto

20
30
tr
tr
spicc.
p
f

Scherzo

60
70

Cantabile

70
80
p
sf
pp
f
dim.
sfmf
sf
mf

Menuetto

Op. 17 No. 3

30
mf
mf
mf
mf
f
f
f
f
p
p
p
p
rit. (2nd time)
rit. (2nd time)
rit. (2nd time)
Trio
p
p
p
p
Fine
p
40
1 3 1
1 1 0 4
1 4 3 1
1
2 1 1 0 4

50
60
rit. (2nd time)
rit. (2nd time)
rit. (2nd time)
rit. (2nd time)
D.C. al Fine

Menuetto

Op. 2 No. 4

Trio
p
4
p
4
p
4
p
f
f
f
f
30
p
p
p
40
tr
tr
p
p
p
p
tr
tr
Menuetto D.C.

A Graceful Dance

Op. 3 No. 4

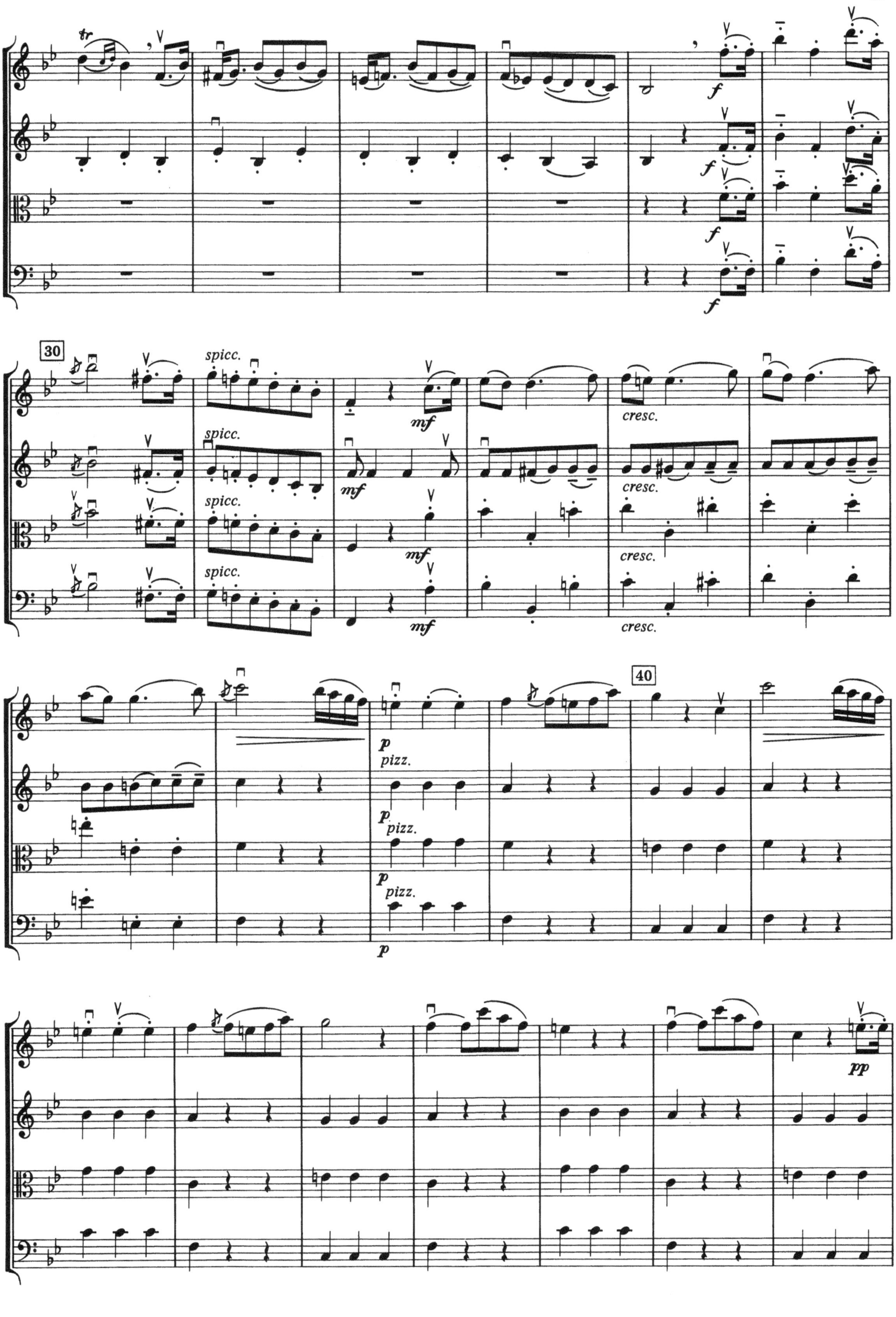

tr
f
30
spicc.
mf
cresc.
40
p
pizz.
pp

130
140
spicc.
spicc.
spicc.
spicc.
cresc.
cresc.
cresc.
cresc.
fp
fp
f
f
f
p
p
p
tr
mf
mf
mf
mf

150
160
pizz.
pizz.
pizz.
pizz.
p
p
p
p
pp
mf arco
mf arco
mf arco
mf
f
f
f
f
p
p
p
p
cresc.
cresc.
cresc.
cresc.

The Horseman

Op. 74 No. 3

30
40
fz
ff
f

50
60
p
p pizzicato
dolce
p

70
col' arco
80
f
f
f
f

110
dim.
dim.
dim.
dim.
p
p
p
p
120
p
cresc.
cresc.
cresc.
fz
fz
fz
ff
ff
ff
ff
Viola
p
p
130
p
p

160
170
sf sf sf
fz fz fz
fz fz fz
fz fz fz
sf ff
fz ff
fz ff
f ff
p
p
p
pizz.
p
1
1
dolce

180
190
col' arco
pp
pp
pp
pp
f
f
f
f
3

The Bird

Op. 33 No. 3

sf
sf
sf
sf
sf
sf
sf
sf
100
dolce
dolce
dolce
dolce
110
cresc.
cresc.
cresc.
cresc.
smorz.
smorz.
cresc.
smorz.
smorz.

150
cresc.
cresc.
cresc.
cresc.
f
f
f
f
p
p
p
p
160
pp
pp
pp
pp
p
p
p
p

Canon

Op. 76 No. 2

30
Trio   spicc.
p
sempre stacc.
spicc.
p
sempre stacc.
40
cresc
cresc
spicc. p   sempre stacc.
cresc
p   sempre stacc.
martelé
f
f
f
f
ff
ff
ff
ff
1.
2.
50
p
p
p
p
1.
p

spicc.
spicc.
spicc.
60
spicc.
70
martelé
cresc
ff
8va
Menuetto D.C.

In the Style of a Minuet

Op. 64 No. 5

30
40
Fine
Trio
p
f

50
60
Menuetto D.C.

Perpetuo Mobile

Op. 64 No. 5

1.
2.
spicc.
f
sf
f
30
sf
sf
sf
f
sf
sf

110
120

Menuetto

30
Fine
Trio
spicc.
p
p
p
p
p
p
40
50
f
f
f
p
p
p
f
Attacca subito il Menuetto